SiMPSONS™
COMICS
CONFIDENTIAL

TITAN BOOKS

SIMPSONS COMICS CONFIDENTIAL

Collects Simpsons Comics 96, 97, 98, 99, and The Simpsons Summer Shindig #2

Copyright © 2012 by
Bongo Entertainment, Inc. All rights reserved.
No part of this book may be used or reproduced in any manner whatsoever
without written permission except in the case of brief quotations
embodied in critical articles and reviews. For information address
Bongo Comics Group c/o Titan Books
P.O. Box 1963, Santa Monica, CA 90406-1963

Published in the UK by Titan Books, a division of Titan Publishing Group Ltd.,
144 Southwark St., London SE1 0UP, under licence from Bongo Entertainment, Inc.

FIRST EDITION: MARCH 2012

ISBN 9780857687364

2 4 6 8 10 9 7 5 3 1

Publisher: Matt Groening
Creative Director: Bill Morrison
Managing Editor: Terry Delegeane
Director of Operations: Robert Zaugh
Art Director: Nathan Kane
Art Director Special Projects: Serban Cristescu
Production Manager: Christopher Ungar
Assistant Art Director: Chia-Hsien Jason Ho
Production/Design: Karen Bates, Nathan Hamill, Art Villanueva
Staff Artist: Mike Rote
Administration: Ruth Waytz, Pete Benson
Editorial Assistant: Max Davison
Legal Guardian: Susan A. Grode

Printed by Quad/Graphics, Inc., Montreal, QC, Canada. 12/13/11

CONTENTS

Homer's Junk Food and Where He Stashes It

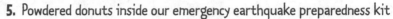

1. Greasy nachos inside the box in the attic marked "Priceless Childhood Memories"
2. Rock candy inside the hide-a-key rock
3. Chocolate coins hidden in a pair of penny loafers
4. Bottle of Rogaine in the shower is filled with maple syrup
5. Powdered donuts inside our emergency earthquake preparedness kit
6. Pork rinds in a hollowed out copy of "The South Beach Diet"
7. Marshmallow Peeps tucked inside a set of Russian nesting dolls
8. Salt water taffy in the gas tank of Flanders' lawnmower (in Homer's garage)
9. Sheets of puff pastry inside the piano bench
10. Packs of bacon taped up inside the fireplace (hoping Santa doesn't get to it first)
11. Pigs in a blanket wedged between couch cushions
12. Chocolate bunnies inside Maggie's Happy Little Elves stuffed animals
13. Bugles corn chips in Lisa's saxophone

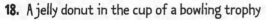
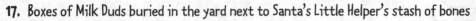

14. Butterscotch candies in his secret safety deposit box at the bank (The passcode is: "gooey." Mmm...gooey.)
15. A box of caramel corn under the Bowflex seat
16. A club sandwich in the VCR tape deck (Who uses that anymore?)
17. Boxes of Milk Duds buried in the yard next to Santa's Little Helper's stash of bones
18. A jelly donut in the cup of a bowling trophy
19. Swedish Fish in the toilet tank at work
20. Chocolate truffles hidden in the dryer's lint trap
21. A wheel of cheese in the car's spare tire compartment
22. The spackle in the tool kit is actually butter
23. A lemon meringue pie on top of the giant Olmec head in the basement
24. Tootsie Rolls in the battery compartment of the old, broken remote
25. Thin Mints hidden between my fat folds

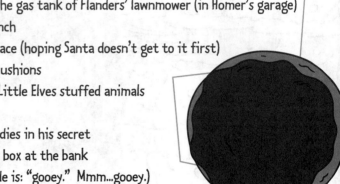

GIVE ME BACK MY GLOBE, BART. I NEED IT FOR *"INTERNATIONAL WEEK"* AT SCHOOL.

DON'T YOU MEAN "MORE BORING THAN USUAL WEEK"?

IT'S *NOT* BORING! INTERNATIONAL WEEK IS SUPPOSED TO BE FUN.

AND YOU'RE *SUPPOSED* TO BE COOL, BUT YOU'RE *NOT*.

HOW COULD A FABULOUSLY HIP KID LIKE ME HAVE SUCH A NERDY SISTER?

OH, POOR, FABULOUS BART! WHAT A HORRIBLE LIFE YOU HAVE!

MAYBE *THIS* WILL TAKE YOUR MIND OFF OF IT!

KICK!

YOWWW!

MUMBLE... MUMBLE...OW!... MUTTER...

STUPID, JERKY, SCHOOL-LOVING NERDETTE! OUCH!

HARD TO *BELIEVE* WE SHARE THE SAME GENE POOL.

WHAT'S YOUR PROBLEM, BOY?

IT'S LISA! WE HAVE NOTHING IN COMMON. ARE YOU SURE SHE'S YOUR DAUGHTER?

GO ASK YOUR MOTHER. AND STOP BLOCKING THE TV!

DON'T YOU LEARN *ANYTHING* IN SCHOOL?

⌐SIGH⌐ FINE!

MOM, ARE YOU SURE *HOMER'S* LISA'S FATHER?

OF COURSE. WHAT KIND OF *QUESTION* IS THAT?

THEN WHY ARE LISA AND I SO *DIFFERENT*?

I MEAN, IT'S NOT LIKE I'M STUPID OR ANYTHING, BUT *SHE* THINKS SCHOOL IS THE GREATEST, AND *I* WAIT FOR THE THREE O'CLOCK BELL LIKE...LIKE A...A KID WAITING FOR CLASS TO LET OUT.

IF THE DIFFERENCE *BOTHERS* YOU, THEN YOU *COULD* TRY TO BE MORE LIKE HER.

NO WAY! I WANT *HER* TO BE MORE LIKE *ME*!

DROP THE *BAR* A FEW FEET! STOP MAKING ME LOOK LIKE THE FAMILY *LOSER*.

BART, LET ME GIVE YOU SOME *ADVICE*.

PEOPLE WHO AIM FOR NOTHING ARE SURE TO HIT IT.

ACCEPT YOUR LIMITATIONS AND GO BEYOND THEM.

THE WINNER ALWAYS HAS A PROGRAM. THE LOSER ALWAYS HAS AN EXCUSE.

THE WINNER ALWAYS HAS A PROGRAM.

THE LOSER ALWAYS HAS AN EXCUSE.

ACCEPT YOUR LIMITATIONS AND GO BEYOND THEM.

PEOPLE WHO AIM FOR NOTHING ARE SURE TO HIT IT.

WHERE DO YOU *GET* THIS STUFF, MOM?

LATER...

BUT, BART, INTERNATIONAL WEEK IS *FUN*!

≲SIGH≳ YOU *TOO*, MILHOUSE?

YOU GET TO *DRESS UP*! LIKE *HALLOWEEN*!

ONE: NO CANDY.

TWO: IT'S EDUCATIONAL.

I JUST CAN'T GET *INTO* IT.

WHAT DO *I* CARE ABOUT SOMEONE IN ANOTHER COUNTRY?

DID THEY CARE ABOUT *ME* WHEN THEY KICKED MY FAMILY OUT OF JAPAN, BRAZIL, AND AUSTRALIA?

SPEAKING OF AUSTRALIA...I'M GOING AS A *SAMURAI*!

G'DAY, SEÑOR BART-SAN!

≲SIGH≳

THAT EVENING...

"...ON WITH OUR ANNUAL INTERNATIONAL WEEK OPENING PROGRAM!"

"WELCOME TEACHERS, STUDENTS, PARENTS..."

INTERNATIONAL WEEK
IT'S A SMALL ADMISSION FEE AFTER ALL

...*AND* OUR ILLUSTRIOUS SCHOOL SUPERINTENDENT CHALMERS!

GET *ON* WITH IT, SKINNER.

IN THE SPIRIT OF INTERNATIONAL BROTHERHOOD AND UNDERSTANDING, ON WITH IT WE *WILL*...UH... ...*GET.*

IMAGINE, OUR LITTLE GIRL *GRADUATING!*

THIS *ISN'T* A GRADUATION, HOMER. AND LISA'S ONLY *SEVEN.*

NOW *REMEMBER* YOUR LINES AND PLACES, CHILDREN.

AND IF YOU FORGET WHERE YOU ARE IN THE SCRIPT, JUST LOOK TO ONE OF *US.*

CONVICTION, PEOPLE! *CONVICTION!* MAKE THEM *BELIEVE!*

THANK YOU, REX.

BART! WHERE'S YOUR AUTHENTIC NATIVE COSTUME?

THIS IS MY COSTUME. I'M A CANADIAN.

PICK ME UP A DOZEN CRULLERS AT TIM HORTON'S, EH?

THAT'S WHAT YOU WEAR EVERY DAY!

UTER'S WEARING THE SAME THING HE ALWAYS DOES.

DOT'S NOT TRUE! THESE ARE SILESIAN LEDERHOSEN! SEE THE PERIWINKLES?

I'M A DRUG DEALER!

BOY, ARE YOU IN TROUBLE, BART.

NOT AS MUCH AS YOU ARE WHEN YOU GET TO THE PLAYGROUND IN THAT OUTFIT.

WHAT'S THE MATTER WITH MY COSTUME? I'M A SAMURAI.

THEN WHERE'S YOUR SWORD, MADAME BUTTERFLY?

WHA-HA-HA-HA!

WHAT AM I TO DO WITH YOU TWO?

TRY THEM AS *ADULTS*.

THAT'S IF YOU'VE GOT THE *GUTS*, SEYMOUR.

IX-NAY ON THE *IRST*-FAY *AME*-NAYS. *ALMERS*-CHAY IS *ISTENING*-LAY.

SKINNER!

I *MAJORED* IN PIG LATIN AT LOUISIANA STATE!

THE PUNISHMENT MUST BE FAIR BUT...

...HARSH.

I WAS *GOING* TO SAY "EDUCATIONAL."

WHY NOT MAKE THEM ENTER THE HANDS-ACROSS-THE-WORLD *PEN PAL* PROGRAM?

THEY'LL *EACH* WRITE TO A DIFFERENT THIRD WORLD CHILD. THAT ACCOMPLISHES *TWO* GOALS...

...THEY CAN MAKE UP FOR RUINING INTERNATIONAL WEEK ON A *GLOBAL* SCALE.

AND BART WILL *HATE* EVERY SECOND OF IT.

¡GULP!¡

WHAT DO *YOU* THINK, SUPERINTENDENT CHALMERS?

I THINK SOMEONE IN THIS ROOM IS MORE *QUALIFIED* TO BE PRINCIPAL THAN YOU, SKINNER.

OH, SUPERINTENDENT CHALMERS...

THAT WAS *GREAT!* AMAZING SPECIAL *EFFECTS!* I REALLY *BELIEVED* THE WORLD WAS ENDING!

HOMER, IT WASN'T *SUPPOSED* TO GO THAT WAY.

OUR CHILDREN MADE A *MOCKERY* OUT OF THE WHOLE CELEBRATION.

I'M JUST GLAD *KOFI ANNAN* TURNED DOWN HIS INVITATION.

YEAH, BUT WHAT KIND OF PUNISHMENT IS THIS FOR *LISA?*

SHE'LL *LOVE* WRITING TO SOME JERK IN SOME JERKY JERKWATER COUNTRY.

IT'S *STILL* HUMILIATING. YOU'RE *USED* TO BEING SCOLDED BY THE PRINCIPAL. IT'S A NEW *EXPERIENCE* FOR ME.

WELL, MAYBE *BOTH* OF YOU SHOULD LEARN SOMETHING FROM THIS. *BART* COULD LEARN ABOUT LIFE IN ANOTHER LAND, AND *LISA* COULD LEARN, WELL...

HOW TO BE LESS *BORING?*

DAD...!

DON'T WORRY, LISA, YOU'LL ALWAYS BE DADDY'S *FAVORITE* LITTLE BORE.

THE NEXT DAY...

HERE IS YOUR ASSIGNED **PEN PAL** PACKET.

THANK YOU, MISS HOOVER.

REMEMBER, THIS IS A **PUNISHMENT**. YOU ARE **NOT** TO ENJOY IT.

YES, MA'AM.

HMM... INTERESTING.

I HAVE A PEN PAL, TOO.

I CALL HIM "**LEAKY**."

I SEE YOU GOT **YOUR** PACKET TOO, BART.

WHAT **COUNTRY** IS YOUR PEN PAL FROM?

SO **WHAT**?

NONE-OF-YOUR-BEESWAXYLVANIA.

IS THAT NEAR **TURKEY**?

LET ME **SEE**, BART!

I WANT TO **KNOW**!

WHY?

FORGET IT!

FINE! **BE** IMPOSSIBLE!

MOM'S **RIGHT**! YOU'LL NEVER LEARN **ANYTHING**!

SO, WHAT ARE YOU GONNA **WRITE** TO THIS FOREIGN KID?

HOW SHOULD **I** KNOW? SOME LINE OF BULL. ANYTHING TO KEEP **SKINNER** OFF MY BUTT.

Dear Salucca,
My name is Lisa, and I am in the second grade.
    I love playing the saxophone, reading Toni Morrison, and enlightening my fellow Springfieldians on the merits of environmentalism and fairness.

I have never heard of your homeland, but I am very curious about how you live and what your school and family are like.

WHERE **DOES** SHE LIVE ANYWAY?

I HOPE IT'S IN MY UPDATED **ATLAS**.

THERE IT IS.

THE CITY OF **HAGENDAZOPOLIS**. RIGHT BY THE RIVER SCZSK.

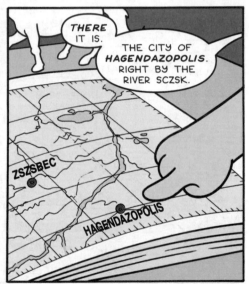

ZSZSBEC

HAGENDAZOPOLIS

HERE'S WHERE HE LIVES. **ZSZSBEC**.

CAN'T THEY AFFORD **VOWELS** IN THIS PLACE? IT'S LIKE TRYING TO READ A VANITY LICENSE PLATE.

ZSZSBEC

HAGENDAZOPOLIS

DO THEY GET **KRUSTY** THERE?

I'M NOT SURE THEY **HAVE** TV.

WOW. THEN WHAT'RE YOU GONNA **WRITE** TO EACH OTHER ABOUT?

LIKE **I** CARE.

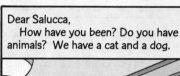

AS DAYS AND WEEKS GO BY...

ANOTHER LETTER FROM SALUCCA!

SHE SURE HAS A ROUGH LIFE. HER MOM AND DAD AND EIGHTEEN SIBLINGS ALL LIVE IN **ONE** ROOM.

IT MUST BE **EASY** TO KEEP HOUSE, THOUGH.

AND THEIR BATHROOM IS **OUTSIDE**.

IN AN **OUTHOUSE**?

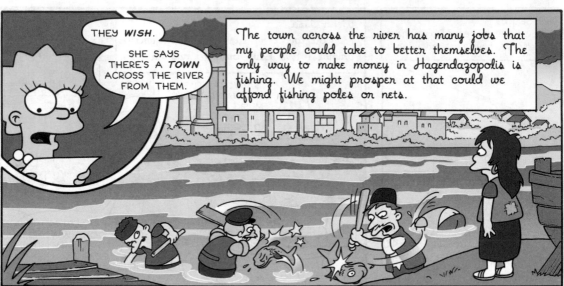

THEY **WISH**.

SHE SAYS THERE'S A **TOWN** ACROSS THE RIVER FROM THEM.

The town across the river has many jobs that my people could take to better themselves. The only way to make money in Hagendazopolis is fishing. We might prosper at that could we afford fishing poles or nets.

HLDUSC VRAVG!

VAVISC?

Once it was our sister city. But many years ago a terrible barge accident destroyed the bridge that once linked our cities.

Sadly, we still cannot reach this town because the government never fixed the bridge that crosses the river Sczsk.

So my people remain poor while our neighbors prosper.

THAT'S *TERRIBLE.* THEY CAN'T REACH THEIR NEIGHBORING COMMUNITY AND *IMPROVE* THEIR LIVES.

IT'S LIKE IF *WE* COULDN'T GO TO SHELBYVILLE.

NOT THAT WE EVER *WOULD.*

"THIS KHAZGULAH KID HAS IT *ROUGH.*"

HE HAS TO WORK ON HIS FAMILY'S FARM *AND* IN A FACTORY MAKING TIVOS.

WHAT'S A TIVO?

HOW SHOULD *I* KNOW?

MY FAVORITE TV SHOW IS ON, AND I'M STUCK HERE SELLING THESE *USELESS* GADGETS. ‡SIGH!‡ GIL *NEVER* GETS A BREAK. ●

WHAT THE HELL IS TIVO?
ASK OUR KNOWLEDGEABLE SALESMAN!

LISTEN TO THIS:

"IT'S DARK WHEN I GET UP IN THE MORNING AND DARK WHEN MY WORK IS DONE AT THE FACTORY. WE CANNOT AFFORD LUXURIES LIKE DAYLIGHT SAVINGS TIME."

GEE.

MAYBE YOU SHOULD *HELP* HIM, BART.

WHAT DO *I* CARE? IT'S NOT *MY* FAULT HE WAS BORN IN A CRUMMY COUNTRY.

BUT MAYBE I *COULD* HELP MAKE HIS LIFE A LITTLE MORE FUN...

THAT EVENING...

DON'T STAY UP TOO *LATE*, LISA.

I'M JUST WRITING TO SALUCCA. I THINK I HAVE THE ANSWER TO THEIR PROBLEMS.

Dear Salucca,
Why do your people wait for your government to re-build the bridge when you could apply to the United States to give you the foreign aid you need to fix it?

"I HAVE DOWN-LOADED THE REQUIRED FORMS TO PETITION OUR GOVERNMENT FOR AID AND ENCLOSED THEM."

AMERICA! WE DO NOT WANT *THEIR* INFLUENCE ON OUR CULTURE!

WITH THEIR *DRIVE-THROUGH* WINDOWS AND *LAWNMOWERS* AND BRITNEY SPEARS *VIDEOS!*

HOW DO *YOU* KNOW ABOUT THESE VIDEOS, PAPA?

UHH...*YUSEF* IN THE VILLAGE TOLD ME, MAMA. HE HAS A SUBSCRIPTION TO MAXIM.

I WILL *COMPLETE* THESE FORMS AND MAIL THEM TO THE AMERICAN PRESIDENT!

HEH HEH HEH...

22

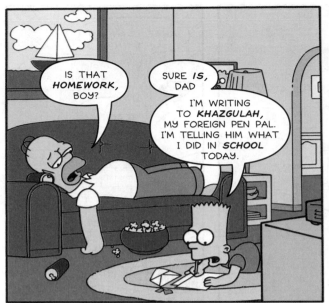

IS THAT **HOMEWORK**, BOY?

SURE **IS**, DAD

I'M WRITING TO **KHAZGULAH**, MY FOREIGN PEN PAL. I'M TELLING HIM WHAT I DID IN **SCHOOL** TODAY.

I HAD A FOREIGN PEN PAL WHEN **I** WAS A BOY.

WHAT COUNTRY WAS HE **FROM**?

MICHIGAN. WHAT A DIFFERENT **WORLD** THEY LIVE IN.

We had science today, and there was an accident.

HEH HEH HEH.

Accidentally on purpose. I let all of the lab animals out of their cages.

After lunch, I got out of a math test by pulling the fire alarm.

BBRRIIING!

And I topped off the day by having some fun with the guy who cuts the lawn at school.

OCH! YE WEE DAFT **BEASTIE**!

WHA HA HA HA!

WHA HA HA HA HA!

KHAZGULAH! NO LAUGHING!

BUT I WAS READING A--

NO READING!

WHAT IS SO HUMOROUS, KHAZ?

MY AMERICAN PEN PAL WRITES OF HIS HI-JINKS AT SCHOOL.

WHAT IS THIS "HI-JINKS"?

HA! HA! HA! HA! HA! HA! HA!

...AND THEN THE TOILETS EXPLODED!

WHAT IS TOILETS?

I SAID NO LAUGHING!

THIRTY SECOND BREAK IS CANCELLED!

WHAT WOULD THIS BART SIMPSON DO IF HE WERE HERE?

FOREMAN YSHMULKO IS MUCH LIKE HIS NEMESIS, SEYMOUR SKINNER.

ONE WONDERS, FAHDUHKA. ONE WONDERS.

THE NEXT DAY...

SOMEONE HAS *DEFACED* THE FACTORY!

WHO WOULD *DO* SUCH A THING?

YOU MUST *INVESTIGATE!*

THE FOLLOWING DAY...

WHO HAS FILLED MY DRAWERS WITH *BOILED CABBAGE?*

THE DAY AFTER THAT...

WHO *IS* IT?

IT IS *GOATS!*

⫶BYAAAAAH!⫶

AND SO ON...

WHO HAS PUT *GLUE* ON MY CHAIR?

I WANT *NAMES!*

ATTENTION, WORKERS!

TAKE THE *REST OF THE DAY OFF!*

YAY!

WHO SAYS THIS?

HOLY DRIKSTAKAH! NO ONE IS HERE!

HEE!

"...AND WHEN HE DISCOVERED THE DEAD FISH IN THE TRUNK OF HIS CAR, HE SCREAMED LIKE A LITTLE GIRL!"

PHWAH-HAH-HAH HAH!

THAT KHAZGULAH'S A *TRUE* CLASS CLOWN.

GOATS! HEE HEE!

AND WHY *NOT*?

HE *LEARNED* FROM THE BEST.

LEARNED *WHAT*, BART? HOW TO GET IN *TROUBLE*?

AND WHAT ARE *YOU* TEACHING *YOUR* PEN PAL, LISA?

WHAT IT'S LIKE TO LIVE IN *GEEKS*VILLE?

HAW HAW!

ACTUALLY, I'M GIVING SUGGESTIONS TO SALUCCA THAT WILL IMPROVE THE LIVES OF *EVERYONE* IN HER VILLAGE.

WHAT? YOU'RE PROMISING NEVER TO *VISIT* HER?

HA!

HA! HA! HA!

HA!

GOATS!

GRRRRR...

26

WHAT'S **THIS** ON MY DESK?

JUST SOME **STATE** DEPARTMENT BUSINESS, MR. PRESIDENT.

I NEVER **HEARD** OF THIS COUNTRY. SOMETHING ABOUT A **BRIDGE**?

YES, MR PRESIDENT.

WELL, THERE ARE **BOUND** TO BE SOME PEOPLE IN THE USA **DESCENDED** FROM IMMIGRANTS FROM THIS PLACE.

I **SUPPOSE**, BUT IT WOULD BE...

... A DARNED **SHAME** TO LOSE THOSE VOTES.

I BELIEVE A GOOD WILL GESTURE IS IN ORDER!

YES, SIR.

LET'S **DO** SOMETHING FOR ALL THE **WHATSIS-AMERICANS** THAT THEY'LL **REMEMBER** ON ELECTION DAY...

YES, SIR.

...BEFORE JIMMY CARTER GETS OUT HIS TOOLBOX AND SHOWS US **ALL** UP!

CONSEQUENTLY...

NEXT ON THE AGENDA ...AN APPROPRIATIONS BILL FOR A **BRIDGE** TO BE BUILT IN...

...I'VE NEVER **HEARD** OF THIS COUNTRY.

MAYBE IT'S ONE OF THE COUNTRIES THAT DOESN'T **HATE** US YET!

LET'S PUT IT TO A **VOTE** THEN.

WOW, TWO LETTERS FROM SALUCCA IN ONE DAY! SHE SAYS THAT THE UNITED STATES GOVERNMENT ARRIVED IN HER VILLAGE WITH *BRIDGE*-BUILDING EQUIPMENT!

LET ME SEE THE REST OF THE MAIL, LISA.

BART GOT A LETTER FROM *HIS* PEN PAL TOO.

SHE SAYS "I HAVE NEVER SEEN MY PEOPLE SO EXCITED!"

So many trucks! All activity stopped like it was the feast of Saint Plzsku!

IS THERE A *SALUCCA BRZUPKSCK* HERE?

THAT IS *ME!*

WE GOT THE *BRIDGE* YOU ORDERED.

SIGN HERE.

HERE.

INITIAL HERE.

SIGN HERE.

We owe all of this to you, Lisa Simpson. Your name is spoken with much respect and admiration throughout our village.

ZK ♥ LISÄ!

ZK ♥ LISÄ!

ZK ♥ LISÄ!

In only a few days we will be able to cross over the river to our estranged sister city.

Then we will pull ourselves up from our misery.

"MANY THANK YOUS. ALL OF OUR FUTURE GOOD FORTUNE IS BECAUSE OF YOU."

OKAY! *OKAY!* YOU READ IT A *MILLION* TIMES ALREADY!

THAT'S *ENOUGH* OF YOUR SOUR GRAPES, YOUNG MAN.

AND YOU GOT A LETTER FROM *YOUR* LITTLE FOREIGN FRIEND, BART.

ALL RIGHT! I WONDER WHAT HE'S *UP* TO!

MMM...SOUR GRAPES.

I have played many of the pranks you have suggested. They were quite funny, and everyone laughed.

HEH HEH.

But yesterday the factory foreman lost his mind, and the police had to come.

YAAAH! STAY AWAY!

As they were taking him away to the sanitarium, a limousine pulled up to the factory.

NO *TALKING!* NO *TALKING!* YEE HEE HEE!

They were from the head office. They closed the plant for falling behind production schedules. Now we have no jobs.

PLANT CLOSED PWZSK XLUQAX

SO, WHAT DOES YOUR FRIEND SAY?

UM...NOT MUCH. KIND OF A DULL DAY IN OLD ZSZSBEC.

WHY DON'T YOU READ YOUR SECOND LETTER, LIS?

ALL RIGHT. "THE DAY HAD COME WHEN THE BRIDGE WAS PREPARED TO BE OPENED, AND THERE WAS MUCH REJOICING."

"OUR CITIES WERE ABOUT TO BE RE-UNITED."

The mayor was to open the bridge officially, and the entire village was there awaiting the prosperity to come.

All that my people could think of were the many jobs and opportunities awaiting them in Zszsbec.

But that is when we saw the people of our sister city fleeing across the new bridge in our direction.

Then they told us of their own terrible woes.

ARE THERE ANY JOBS IN HAGENDAZOPOLIS?

THERE IS NO WORK! THE TIVO FACTORY IS CLOSED!

BUT WE WERE COMING TO YOUR CITY FOR WORK.

WHAT IS TIVO?

Now both of our villages make the long trek to Spliskatisgrad where we hear they make George Foreman grills.

It may be a while before I can write to you again...

"...WE HAD TO EAT OUR POSTAGE STAMPS FOR THE NOURISHING GLUE."

THIS IS *TERRIBLE!*

I DUNNO, LISA. LENNY *LOVES* HIS GEORGE FOREMAN GRILL.

THAT'S THE BREAKS, SIS.

WAIT A MINUTE...YOU SAID *YOUR* PEN PAL IS FROM *ZSZSBEC!*

I *DID?*

THAT'S THE VILLAGE *ACROSS* THE RIVER FROM SALUCCA'S.

WHAT A *CO-WINKYDINK,* HUH?

YOU AND DISASTER ARE *NEVER* A CO-WINKYDINK, BART.

SHOW ME YOUR *LETTER!*

UM... MAYBE *LATER,* OKAY?

I *KNEW* IT!

MOM!

TAKE IT *OUTSIDE!*

IT'S *GREAT* TO SEE THEM SO INVOLVED IN A SCHOOL PROJECT, HOMER.

ESPECIALLY ≥MFFH≥ WHEN THEY LEAVE ≥CHMFF≥ THE TABLE ≥SMAK≥ IN THE MIDDLE OF *DINNER!*

WELL, NOW THAT *YOU'RE* HERE THIS IS OFFICIALLY THE *WORST...PARTY...EVER!*

AH HEE HEE HEE!

A T S U V I RNXQ ZYBOM GROENING

ACH! THIS PUNCH TASTES LIKE SCOTTISH BOG WATER!

AND THESE NACHO CHIPS ARE AS DISAPPOINTING AS MY SON SEYMOUR!

HRMMM...

HRMMM...

THIS WAS A WONDERFUL IDEA, DR. HIBBERT. A "COME AS YOUR *NEIGHBOR*" COSTUME PARTY, RIGHT HERE IN YOUR OFFICE!

HEY, FLANDERS! WHERE'S YOUR *COSTUME*?! YOU'RE SUPPOSED TO BE A NEIGHBOR!

I'M DRESSED AS MR. ROGERS.

HE WAS *EVERYBODY'S* NEIGHBOR!

AND NOW A LITTLE SURPRISE!

GREAT! OL' GIL *LOVES* SURPRISES.

WHAT IS IT? FOOD? A GAME? DANCING GIRLS?

BETTER! YOUR ANNUAL *FLU SHOTS!*

GASP!

NONE OF YOU CAME IN FOR THEM THIS YEAR.

GET YOUR FLU SHOT!

MAYBE IT WAS OUR NEW MASCOT, *SCREAMY THE FLU SHOT BEAR!*

SO I MADE UP THIS FAKE PARTY!

NOW ROLL UP YOUR SLEEVES AND GET IN LINE!

OH FOR HEAVEN'S SAKE, YOU *NERVOUS NELLIES!*

I'LL GO FIRST!

WHAT'S WITH THE TATTOO?

OH, THAT'S FROM YEARS AGO WHEN HOMER AND I WENT TO *NEW ORLEANS* FOR *MARDI GRAS.*

THE *LESS* SAID ABOUT THAT WEEKEND THE *BETTER!*

¡GASP!¡

STAB!

36

THE NEXT DAY...

...AND ːGROANː WHEN I FINALLY CAME TO IN THE MORNING I WAS IN THE *GUTTER!*

IT WAS SURPRISINGLY COMFORTABLE.

YEAH, AFTER THE TENTH TIME I WOKE UP IN IT I HAD THE GUTTER PADDED!

THE INDIVIDUAL COIL SUPPORT REALLY GIVES YOU A GOOD NIGHT'S SLEEP!

THANKS FOR WATCHING RODDY AND TODDY WHILE I WAS IN MY FEVER DREAM.

THEY LET ROD PUT *SYRUP* ON HIS *TOASTER PASTRY!*

BEEP-BEEP! I'M *THE ROAD RUNNER!*

OKAY, BOYS, GET IN THE FLANDERS-MOBILE! WE'RE GOING ON A TRIP!

YOU'RE *STILL* DOING THAT?

OH YES. IT MAY HAVE BEEN A HALLUCINATION, BUT THE ADVICE WAS STILL GOOD. THE BOYS ARE TOO SHELTERED.

NOW I'M *THE TASMANIAN DEVIL!*

DADDY! ROD SAID HE'S *THE DEVIL!* I'LL GET THE HOLY WATER!

SO WHERE ARE YOU GOING?

WHEREVER THE ROAD TAKES US!

AS LONG AS IT'S ONE OF THE BLUE, BILLY GRAHAM-APPROVED, FAMILY VALUES STATES!

NED, AS YOUR **BEST FRIEND**, I FEEL IT'S MY **DUTY** WHILE YOU'RE GONE TO LOOK AFTER YOUR **BUMPER POOL TABLE, BIG SCREEN TV,** AND **IMPORTED BEER BAR!**

OH, I'VE GOT THAT COVERED, HOMER! I MADE A COUPLE OF CALLS, AND I'M DONATING MY HOME TO THE POOR WHILE I'M GONE.

THEY TAKE SOMEONE OUT OF A FILTHY SHACK AND LET THEM HOUSESIT IN THE SUBURBS.

IT'S CALLED THE **LOVE SHACK** PROGRAM!

SO WHO'LL BE LIVING THERE?

PLEASE LET IT BE WILLIE! PLEASE LET IT BE WILLIE!

AND SO, THE NEXT DAY...

♪ WHAT'S NEW, PUSSYCAT? ♪

♪ MEOW ♪ MEOW MEOW ♪ MEOW! ♪

¡SIGH!¿

UM...EXCUSE ME. *BRANDINE*, IS IT?

IT BE!

I DON'T MIND YOU USING MY CLOTHESLINE, BUT COULD YOU PLEASE NOT PUT *YOUR* CLOTHES ON TOP OF *MY CLEAN ONES* TO DRY?

THEY AIN'T DRYING. I'M JEST RESTIN' 'EM THERE SO THAT THEY SOAK UP SOME O' THAT NICE *LAUNDRY SOAP* SMELL.

IT'S EASIER THAN CLEANIN'!

HRMMM...

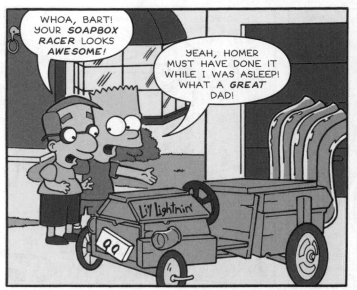

WHOA, BART! YOUR *SOAPBOX RACER* LOOKS *AWESOME!*

YEAH, HOMER MUST HAVE DONE IT WHILE I WAS ASLEEP! WHAT A *GREAT* DAD!

MY DAD DOES STUFF FOR ME, TOO.

LIKE WHAT?

WELL, ER...UM...

AN HOUR LATER...

UM...HE SHARED A *CIGAR* WITH ME ONCE!

C'MON, MILHOUSE, WE'RE BURNING DAYLIGHT HERE!

ONE SHORT TRIP LATER...

THIS *ABANDONED FLINT QUARRY* IS THE PERFECT PLACE TO TRY OUT THE RACER!

NOW PUSH, MIL-MAN! *PUSH!*

SPARK!

FWOOOOOOSH!!

AAAAAAAAAAH!

WE CLOCKED THE VEHICLE GOING 90 MILES PER HOUR, AND THE CAR REEKS OF BOOZE!

WOW! I MUST HAVE REALLY TIED ONE ON, BECAUSE I DON'T REMEMBER *ANY* OF THAT!

NOT *YOU!* IT WAS YOUR BOY, BART!

BART! WHAT DID I TELL YOU ABOUT *DRINKING AND DRIVING?*

NOTHING, I'M ONLY TEN! I CAN'T DRINK *OR* DRIVE!

TOUCHÉ!

HEY, CHIEF, CHECK THIS OUT!

THE BACKEND OF THE SOAPBOX RACER WAS TURNED INTO A *STILL!*

A FEW MOMENTS LATER...

CLETUS! HOW COULD YOU TURN MY BOY'S INNOCENT *SOAPBOX RACER* INTO A *STILL...*

...WITHOUT OFFERING ME *ANY* OF THAT *SWEET, SWEET MOON-SHINE?!*

WELL, Y'ALL DONE STOLE MY PRIZE PIG, *SQUEALY DAN!*

DON'T TRY TO *CHANGE* THE SUBJECT!

SQUEEEE!

YOU ARE THE *WORST NEIGHBOR EVER!*

DO YOU *MIND?* I'M TALKING TO CLETUS HERE!

OKAY, BUT CLOSE YOUR ROBE WHEN YOU GET THE NEWSPAPER, AND I NEED YOU TO RETURN THE *KIDNEY DIALYSIS MACHINE* YOU BORROWED!

I WANT YOU OFF'N MY PROPERTY BY THE TIME I COUNT AS HIGH AS I KIN COUNT!

OR *WHAT?* YOU'LL SHOOT ME FULL OF *BUCKSHOT?*

NOPE. THE CITY WON'T LET ME OWN FIREARMS BECAUSE O' MY *RECKLESS NATURE* AND *CRIMINAL RECORD!*

YEAH, ME TOO. LOUSY GOVERNMENT!

MR. SIMPSON, I'M HERMAN OF *HERMAN'S MILITARY ANTIQUES AND BATTLE SUPPLIES*.

I UNDERSTAND YOU'RE HAVING A FEUD WITH YOUR NEIGHBOR!

WHAT? HOW'D YOU FIND OUT SO FAST?

THE INTERNET!

NOW, I KNOW YOU BOTH CAN'T USE GUNS, SO MAY I SUGGEST YOU LET ME SUPPLY YOU WITH THE NEXT BEST THING?

THE SPLATTER SHOT 5000!

WAR MANUAL

A *PAINT-BALL GUN?* I DON'T KNOW, HOMER!

SPLAT!

BLAM!

OH, DID I MENTION I ALREADY SOLD ONE TO CLETUS ALONG WITH *TEN BOXES* OF REFILL CARTRIDGES?

WE'LL TAKE *TWENTY!*

THE NEXT WEEK...

MOM! THE SCHOOL BUS IS HERE!

HOMER! THE KIDS NEED COVER FIRE!

PTUUU!

THWACK!

PTUUU!

AAAAAAH!

SPLORT!

SPRINGFIELD ELE SCHOOL

48

LATER THAT AFTERNOON...

THWACK!

THWACK!

HOW WAS SCHOOL, LISA?

GOOD, MOM!

I'LL BE IN THE TUB SOAKING IN *TURPENTINE* IF YOU NEED ME!

SAVE SOME FOR YOUR *BROTHER*!

BAAAAH!

AAAAAH!

SHHHHH!

YAAAA!

DON'T BE SCARED! THE NAME'S Q-BERT! OLD FRANNIE HERE WANDERED INTO YOUR HOUSE, AND I SNUCK IN TO GET HER BACK!

THAT'S NO EXCUSE FOR BREAKING AND...

HER *BABIES* NEEDED HER!

AW! THEY ARE SO CUTE!

BAAAAH!

I LOOK AFTER **ALL OUR CRITTERS!**

IT'S BEEN REALLY HARD WHAT WITH ALL OUR FAMILIES **FUSSIN'** AND A' **FIGHTIN'!**

WISH I HAD SOME HELP, BUT MY BROTHERS AND SISTERS JUST DON'T COTTON TO ANIMALS.

I **LOVE** ANIMALS! I CAN HELP!

NO, IT'S TOO DANGEROUS! YOU'D BE SPOTTED RIGHT AWAY!

I HAVE AN IDEA! MEET ME IN YOUR BACKYARD!

MINUTES LATER...

SEE? I JUST TOOK SOME OF THE CLOTHES YOUR MOM PUT ON OUR CLOTHESLINE!

GOSH, THAT'S **CLEVER!**

YOU'RE AS **SMART** AS YOU ARE **PURTY!**

YOU'RE MAKING ME BLUSH!

AND ITCH!

NO, THAT'D BE THE CHIGGERS IN THE CLOTHES.

OH...YEAH! HEH HEH!

SCRITCH!

SCRITCH!

MEANWHILE, AT THE ANDROID'S DUNGEON...

COMING NEXT MONTH: RADIOACTIVE MAN VS. HIS OWN SELF-LOATHING

ITCHY

BONGO CLASSICS

NO CHECKS!

MARVEY HEROES

DEE CEE CARDS

COMIC BOOK GUY? WHAT HAPPENED?

I HAD THE MISFORTUNE OF BEING CAUGHT IN THE *CROSSFIRE* BETWEEN YOUR FATHER AND CLETUS THIS MORNING.

OH, MAN, I'M SO SORRY.

NO NEED FOR APOLOGIES! IT SAVED ME PURCHASING A COSTUME FOR TONIGHT'S *CLASSIC STAR TREK MASQUERADE BALL* BY MIMICKING *FRANK GORSHIN* IN EPISODE #70 OF THE ORIGINAL SERIES!

"LET THAT BE YOUR LAST BATTLEFIELD." *PREACHIEST* STAR TREK *EVER!*

LATER...

THIS HAS BEEN SO MUCH FUN, BUT I SHOULD BE HEADING HOME!

OKAY, SEE YOU TOMORROW FOR THE 5 A.M. *HOG SLOPPIN'?*

I WOULDN'T MISS IT!

KISS!

HEY, BROTHER AND SISTER, QUIT PERPETUATING AN OFFENSIVE HILLBILLY *STEREOTYPE!*

THAT NIGHT...

PSSSST! LISA!

Q~BERT! HOW DID YOU *GET* UP THERE?

THE ANNOTATED NANCY DREW

I HAD ME A LITTLE HELP!

OINK!

OINK!

BAAA!

MOO!

YOU DIDN'T COME BY FOR THE EVENIN' YAK MILKIN'.

I KNOW...SORRY. I'M JUST *WORRIED* WE'RE GOING TO GET *CAUGHT*!

AW, THAT'LL NEVER HAPPEN! NOW HOW 'BOUT A GOOD-NIGHT KISS?

I DONE *FLOSSED* MY TEETH WITH FRESH *HAY*!

WELL... OKAY.

LISA, YOUR DINNER'S--

WHAT THE #*@?!

HEY! KEEP DOWN THE SWEARAGE! THERE BE IMPRESSIONABLE YOUNGUN'S LISTENIN' THAT--

NO! I CAIN'T BELIEVE MY EYE-HOLES! BOY, ONCE I REMEMBER WHICH ONE YOU IS, YOU'RE GONNA BE IN A HEAP O' TROUBLE!

I CAN EXPLAIN! IT'S ALL **MY** FAULT!

TELL IT TO THE **JUDGE!**

ONE TRIP TO THE COURTHOUSE LATER...

I DON'T KNOW WHY YOU DRAGGED ME AWAY FROM DINNER FOR THIS!

THERE'S GOTTA BE **SOME** LAW HE'S BROKE THAT YOU CAN PUT HIM AND HIS FAMILY AWAY FOR!

THERE'S A MISDEMEANOR ABOUT **FARM ANIMAL STACKING**, BUT, FRANKLY, I THINK YOU SHOULD JUST SETTLE YOUR PROBLEMS YOURSELF, SO I CAN GET HOME BEFORE MY ROAST BEEF GETS COLD.

MORE **FEUDIN'** IT IS!

GET MY PAINT GUN, BOY!

WHILE YOU WERE WASTING JUDGE SNYDER'S TIME, I WAS TRYING TO FIND A WAY TO END THIS FIGHT BY LOOKING IN THE CITY RECORDS!

DO THEY HAVE **"JIMMY CRACK CORN"** ON **78**? THAT BE MY FA-VOR-RITE!

I FOUND BOTH OF OUR FAMILY TREES! IF YOU GO BACK TO THE MID-1800S, THEY *CONNECT*. WE'RE ALL ACTUALLY SECOND COUSINS THREE TIMES REMOVED!

HUH?

WHAT?

IT BE *TRUE!* AND THE UNWRITTEN *COUNTRY CODE* STATES THAT THERE CAIN'T BE NO FEUDIN' BETWEEN *KINFOLK!* IT JUST AIN'T RIGHT!

I AGREE! I'D *NEVER* BE ABLE TO HURT A FAMILY MEMBER!

HOW ABOUT ALL THE TIMES YOU CHOKED ME?

THOSE WERE JUST *NECK HUGS!*

COME HERE, *COUSIN!*

GAWRSH!

NOW THAT WE'RE RELATED, I GUESS WE'LL HAVE TO JUST BE FRIENDS!

ACTUALLY, I DON'T HAVE A PROBLEM WITH...

I GUESS WE'LL HAVE TO *JUST BE FRIENDS!*

YES'M!

AND SO...

MORE *MOONSHINE*, COUSIN?

YOU GOT IT, COUSIN!

YOU KNOW, IT'S NICE HAVING THINGS ALL PEACEFUL LIKE THIS!

IT *RIGHTLY* IS!

I GOTTA SAY THOUGH, I KINDA MISS THE EXCITEMENT OF THE FEUD.

IT DID GET THE HEARTBONE A' PALPITATIN'!

BUT I GUESS THEM DAYS IS GONE FOREVER!

ERT!

HOMER! CLETUS! GOOD TO SEE YOU BOTH! OH, WE HAD A GREAT TIME ON OUR TRIP, AND WE'VE GOT *HOURS* OF *SLIDES* TO SHOW YOU!

THOSE SOUND LIKE *FIGHTIN' WORDS* TO ME! HOW ABOUT *YOU*, COUSIN?

THEY SURELY DO!

THE SIMPSONS au NATUREL!

JAMES W. BATES
SCRIPT

MARCOS ASPREC
PENCILS

STEVE STEERE, JR.
INKS

ART VILLANUEVA
COLORS

KAREN BATES
LETTERS

BILL MORRISON
EDITOR

MATT GROENING

MMM... PORK CHOP NIGHT.

HI, HOMIE.

WHERE ARE THE PORK CHOPS?

DID *THE BOY* EAT MY PORK CHOPS AGAIN?

NO.

THE GIRL?

NO ONE ATE YOUR PORK CHOPS. I DIDN'T PUT THEM OUT YET BECAUSE I DIDN'T WANT YOU DISTRACTED.

DISTRACTED? FROM WHAT?

OUR "FAMILY MEETING" TO DISCUSS THE PREPARATIONS FOR OUR *VACATION* NEXT WEEK!

D'OH! I *KNEW* THERE WAS A REASON I WANTED TO GO TO MOE'S INSTEAD OF COMING HOME FOR PORK CHOPS!

"PREPARATIONS" SOUNDS LIKE WORK! ISN'T VACATION AN *ESCAPE* FROM WORK?

HERE, DAD. THIS IS THE BROCHURE. I'VE CIRCLED THE CAMP ACTIVITIES I THINK WE SHOULD SIGN UP FOR!

BACK 2 NATURE CAMP, HUH? AREN'T WE GOING TO MONSTER TRUCKVILLE?

NO, *LISA* GOT TO PICK. MONSTER TRUCKVILLE WAS *MY* IDEA!

THAT'S RIGHT, WE HAD A DEAL! YOU SAID IF I MAKE STRAIGHT "A"s, I GET TO PICK THE NEXT FAMILY VACATION.

WHY'D I EVER MAKE SUCH A SUCKER DEAL WITH LISA? SHE'S THE *SMART* ONE!

IT MUST HAVE BEEN THAT SIX-PACK OF DUFF TALKING.

OH, DUFF! YOU AND YOUR BIG MOUTH!

I'M WORRIED THOUGH. I TRIED TO PRE-REGISTER FOR A TIMESLOT TO FEED THE BABY DEER, BUT THERE WAS SOME KIND OF SNAFU. THEY COULDN'T FIND OUR RESERVATIONS.

DON'T WORRY, LISA. YOUR FATHER TOOK OUR VACATION FUND TO THE TRAVEL AGENCY OVER A MONTH AGO.

OOH. ABOUT THAT...

ONE MONTH AGO...

FAT TONY'S PET GROOMING CENTER

SPRINGFIELD TRAVEL

TODAY! INTERSPECIES WRESTLING CHAMPIONSHIP: HUNGRY TIGER VERSUS KARATE MONKEY BETTING REQUIRED

TALK ABOUT EASY MONEY! THAT MONKEY WON'T LAST TWO MINUTES!

THREE MINUTES LATER...

A PLEASURE DOIN' BUSINESS WIT' YOU.

ARE YOU SURE THAT WAS A TIGER? I THINK IT WAS JUST A FAT HOUSE CAT?

BACK TO THE PRESENT...

HOMER, IS SOMETHING WRONG? YOU JUST MUMBLED SOMETHING ABOUT A MONKEY KICKING LIKE CHUCK NORRIS.

ER...I'M JUST SO EXCITED ABOUT BACK 2 NATURE CAMP...YEAH...MAYBE THEY'LL HAVE MONKEYS THERE!

KEEP SMILING...NOBODY WILL KNOW...KEEP SMILING...STUPID MONKEY!

OH, DAD. THANK YOU, THANK YOU, THANK YOU! THIS IS GOING TO BE THE *BEST* VACATION *EVER!*

SPRINGFIELD TRAVEL

DISCOUNTS FOR WITNESS PROTECTION PROGRAM MEMBERS COME ON IN WE'LL TAKE CARE OF YOU.

I ONLY HAVE FIFTY-TWO DOLLARS, BUT MY FAMILY NEEDS TO GO TO BACK 2 NATURE CAMP.

FIFTY-TWO BUCKS? BUDDY, FOR THAT MONEY THE CLOSEST I CAN COME TO GETTING YOU BACK TO NATURE WOULD BE FOR ME TO BEAT YOU SENSELESS WITH THIS POTTED PLANT.

SHORTLY...

HOLD ON, MISTER. IF OL' GIL DOESN'T MAKE A DEAL TODAY, THEY'RE GONNA *FIRE* ME! *I'LL* FIND YOU SOMETHING.

REALLY?

THERE WAS A LAST MINUTE CANCELLATION FOR THIS NEW PLACE THAT *SOUNDS* LIKE THE BACK 2 NATURE CAMP. IT'S CALLED *CAMP AU NATUREL*.

NATURAL, HUH?

WHAT'S YOUR BUDGET?

I JUST SPENT MY LAST FIFTY BUCKS.

ISN'T THERE *ANYTHING* IN THAT WALLET?

I HAVE A FREE CAR WASH COUPON AND A "BUY ONE GET ONE FREE" KRUSTY BURGER CERTIFICATE.

WE'VE GOT A DEAL!

THE FAMILY VACATION...

BUT DAD, THIS ISN'T THE *BACK 2 NATURE CAMP!*

LOOKS LIKE A BUNCH OF TREES TO ME.

PARK HERE FOR CAMP

THAT SIGN SAYS "CAMP!"

I'M LINDSEY NAEGLE, YOUR OFFICIAL GREETER TO *CAMP AU NATUREL.* OUR EXCLUSIVE AND LUXURIOUS ACCOMMODATIONS ARE JUST A FEW MILES HIKE THROUGH THE WOODS!

HIKE?

A BRISK HIKE IS THE PERFECT WAY TO GET RID OF THE STRESS OF BIG CITY LIVING.

BIG CITY? *SPRINGFIELD?*

OUR PORTERS WILL TAKE YOUR BAGS. NOT THAT YOU'LL NEED THEM AT CAMP AU NATUREL...HA!

C'MON, SIMPSONS. WHO'S READY TO HIT THE PATH TO THE AU NATUREL WAY OF LIFE?

I AM!

A MILE INTO THE WOODS...

WATCH OUT FOR THE POISON IVY!

I HATE NATURE.

CAN'T HIKE ANYMORE...LEAVE ME...LET THE BABY DEER EAT ME.

A HUNDRED YARDS LATER...

WE'RE ALMOST AT CAMP AU NATUREL BUT BEFORE I INTRODUCE YOU TO THE OTHER CAMPERS, WHY DON'T YOU ALL TAKE A QUICK REFRESHING SHOWER?

I GUESS I AM A LITTLE RIPE.

IF THAT'S *RIPE*, I'D HATE TO SMELL YOU WHEN YOU *GO BAD*.

¡GIGGLE!¿

WHERE'S THE "NO ANIMAL TESTING" LABEL? WHAT'S THE DEAL WITH THIS CAMP?

HO! HO! HO!

HOMER?!? YOU BETTER COME OUT HERE!

HUH?

MARGE! I'M TRYING TO...

...TAKE A SHOW-WA-WA-WHOA! NAKED LADY!

WHY DO I GET THE FEELING WE AREN'T AT THE CAMP LISA WANTED TO GO TO?

WELL...

WHY WOULDN'T LISA WANT TO COME *HERE*? CAMP AU NATUREL IS THE HIGHEST-RATED *NUDIST RESORT* IN THE SPRINGFIELD-SHELBYVILLE AREA!

FOLLOW ME. YOU CAN KEEP THE TOWELS FOR NOW *BUT*...

≡SNICKER≡ SHE SAID "*BUTT!*"

...YOU SIMPLY *MUST* GIVE THE AU NATUREL WAY A TRY!

OOH, I THINK "AU NATUREL" IS FRENCH FOR *NAKED*?

WELCOME TO CAMP AU NATUREL

68

VACATION? DIDN'T YOU TAKE AN OATH?

DOOOH! CURSE YOU, HIPPOCRATES!

YOU'LL BE OKAY. JUST KEEP THE AFFLICTED AREA OUT IN THE FRESH AIR.

WHAT A RELIEF! I COULD HUG YOU.

MY DIAGNOSIS IS NO, YOU COULD *NOT*.

THE DOCTOR'S RIGHT! WHAT I NEED IS FRESH AIR! OH, HOW I'VE SUFFERED UNDER THE OPPRESSION OF BLUE PANTS!

THINK ABOUT HOW MUCH THOSE BLUE PANTS HAVE SUFFERED.

WITHOUT THE SHACKLE-LIKE CONFINEMENTS OF CLOTHING, I CAN EVEN FIGHT OFF MY OVER-WHELMING DESIRE TO STRANGLE THE BOY!

GET OFF!

MARGE, I'M *GLAD* I LOST OUR VACATION FUND BETTING ON INTERSPECIES WRESTLING! I'M *GLAD* I HAD TO TAKE THIS CUT-RATE DEAL!

YOU *WHAT*?

THE NEXT WEEK...

HELLO, MRS. SIMPSON.

COME ON IN.

TO COMPENSATE YOU FOR THE TROUBLE, THE MANAGEMENT OF CAMP AU NATUREL AND SPRINGFIELD TRAVEL HAVE MADE THE ARRANGEMENTS FOR YOUR ENTIRE FAMILY TO SPEND AN ALL-EXPENSES PAID V.I.P. WEEK AT THE BACK 2 NATURE CAMP.

BACK 2 NATURE CAMP

REALLY?

IT'S THE LEAST WE CAN DO AFTER ALL YOUR TROUBLE.

BACK 2 NATURE CAMP

GREAT. I CAN'T WAIT TO FAWN OVER THE BABY DEER.

THOSE RESERVATIONS HAVE NO EXPIRATION SO YOU CAN WAIT UNTIL MR. SIMPSON IS...READY.

BACK 2 NATURE CAMP

HOW IS HE, BY THE WAY?

SEE FOR YOURSELF.

I BROUGHT YOU THE SCARF YOU WANTED.

GIMME!

CLOTHES GOOD. NAKED BAD. LAYERS GOOD. MORE CLOTHES. NO SKIN. NO PATTY. NO SELMA.

IT'S THE END, MAN!

FIN

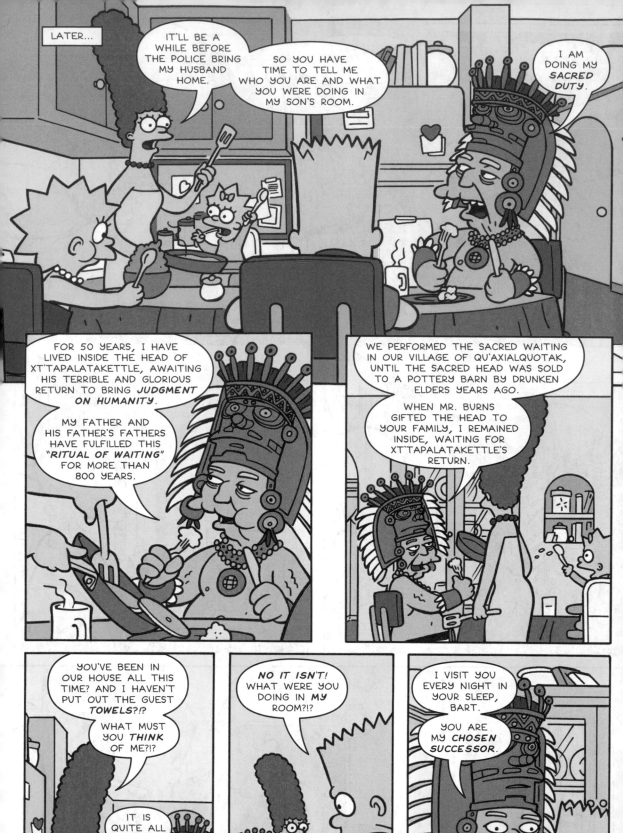

I AM OLD, AND I HAVE NO SON TO CARRY ON THE SACRED WAITING, SO I HAVE BEEN DESPERATELY PLANTING THAT SUGGESTION IN *YOUR* SLEEPING MIND FOR MONTHS.

WHAAAT!?!

IT CERTAINLY EXPLAINS ALL THE JEWELRY YOU'VE STARTED WEARING.

DON'T BE A HATER, LISA...IT'S JUST MY *BLING BLING*.

WAIT A MINUTE...THIS BLING BLING IS MADE OF *ROCK!*

MOM!! DO SOMETHING!

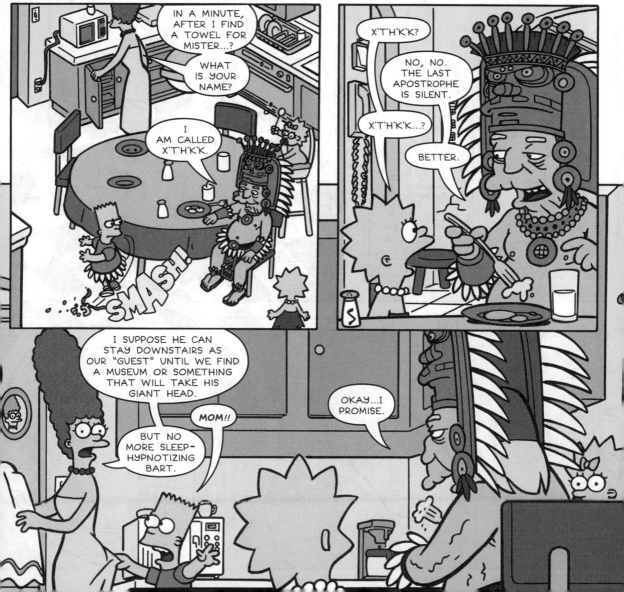

IN A MINUTE, AFTER I FIND A TOWEL FOR MISTER...?

WHAT IS YOUR NAME?

I AM CALLED X'T'H'K'K.

SMASH!

X'T'H'K'K?

NO, NO. THE LAST APOSTROPHE IS SILENT.

X'T'H'K'K...?

BETTER.

I SUPPOSE HE CAN STAY DOWNSTAIRS AS OUR "GUEST" UNTIL WE FIND A MUSEUM OR SOMETHING THAT WILL TAKE HIS GIANT HEAD.

MOM!!

BUT NO MORE SLEEP-HYPNOTIZING BART.

OKAY...I PROMISE.

LEAVE ME ALONE.

WE CANNOT TALK WHEN YOU ARE ASLEEP, SO THIS IS A GOOD TIME FOR ME.

I CAN'T SEE PAST THE FEATHERS.

YOU WOULD BE ALLOWED TO PLAY VIDEO GAMES WHILE YOU DID THE SACRED WAITING, O CHOSEN ONE. THERE ARE VERY FEW RULES, ACTUALLY.

I DON'T WANT TO BE YOUR STUPID CHOSEN ONE!

COME WITH ME AND JUST SIT IN THE HEAD, TELL ME WHAT YOU THINK...

NO!

MARGE! I'M HOME!

HOMER! WHAT HAPPENED WHEN YOU GOT TO THE PLANT NAKED?

AHHH... EVERYBODY SCREAMED FOR A WHILE.

THEN THEY THREW TOWELS OVER ME.

AND THEN I DROVE HOME...

...EXACTLY WHAT HAPPENS WHEN I DO THIS WHEN I'M AWAKE!

LOUSY DREAM!

YOU KNOW, IK-THICK-KICK...IF ALL YOU NEED OUT OF YOUR CHOSEN ONE IS SOMEONE TO SIT ON HIS BUTT FOR THE REST OF HIS LIFE AND DO NOTHING...

...HOMER'S YOUR MAN.

AND TV GUIDES!

WOO-HOO!

TV GUIDE — KRUSTY'S **100TH** EPISODE — *PANT!!* — *PANT!!* 25 YEARS AND STILL GOING

TV GUIDE — **IT'S GABBO!** — HE'LL BE H... A GOOD L... TIME FO...

THIS DREAMING STUFF IS FINALLY STARTING TO PAY OFF.

TAKE *THAT*, CONSCIOUS THOUGHT!

WUH-OH.

NOW EVERY-THING'S GETTING ALL "FREUD-EY IMAGEY."

THE GIANT HEAD CLEARLY WANTS TO *EAT* ME.

BUT IT OFFERS *DONUTS* AND I...I...

NO! THIS IS *MY* FANTASY!

AND I DON'T HAVE TO DO WHAT THE *GIANT HEAD* SAYS!

I CAN FOLLOW MY *OWN* PATH OF DESTINY!

SO I'M DRIVING TO THE DUFF BREWERY NAKED!!

D'OH!

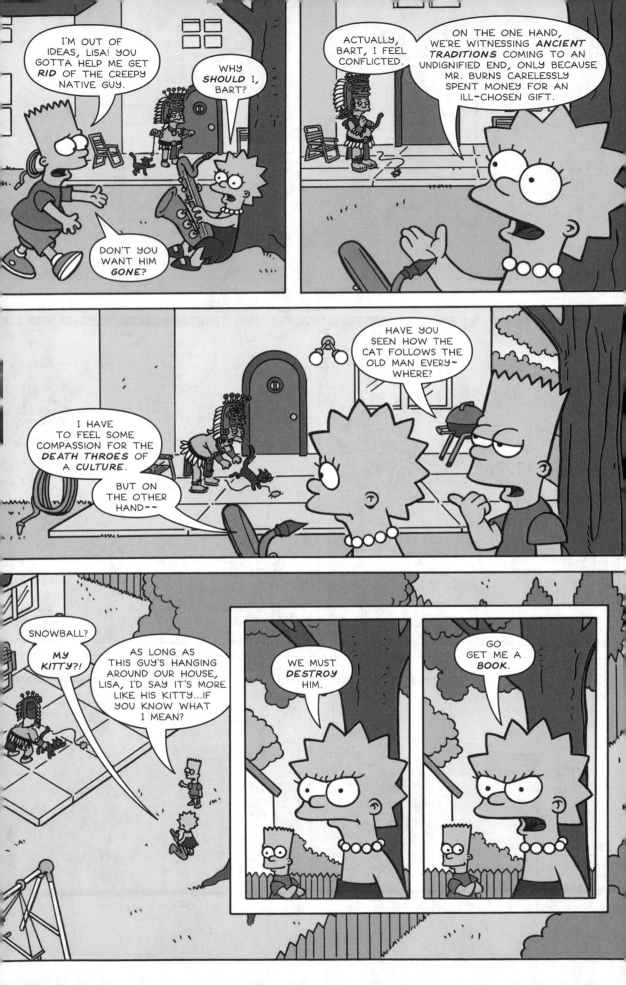

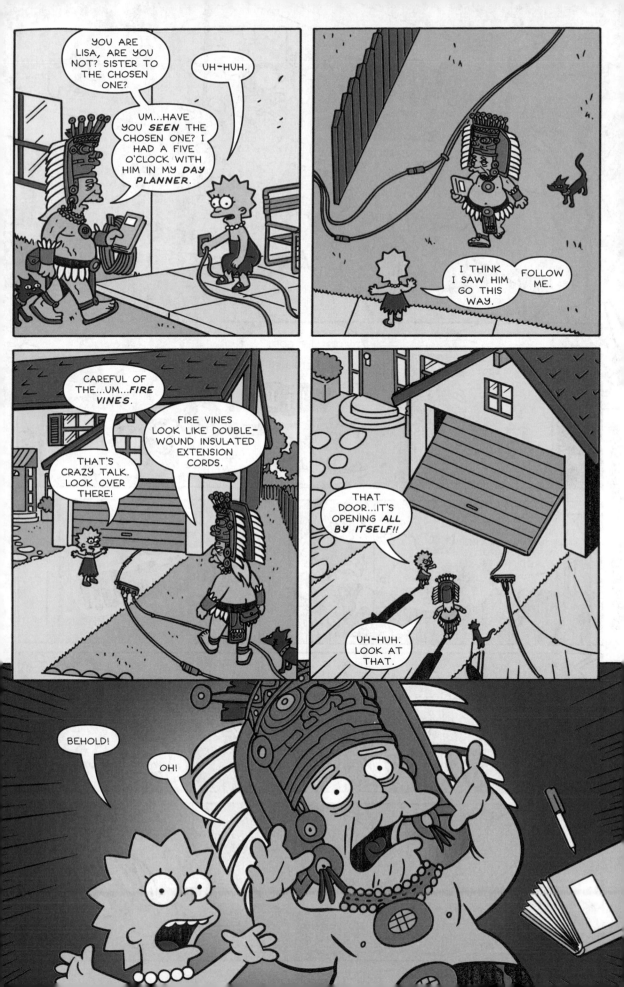

WITHOUT THE FLAMES, IT IS HARD TO BE CONVINCED.

BUT I HAVE WAITED A LIFETIME...SO I WILL KEEP AN OPEN MIND.

OOOOHHHH

I AM YOUR GLORIOUS AND TERRIBLE LORD!

ALL RIGHT, XT'TAPALATA-KETTLE... ...WHAT IS YOUR *JUDGMENT UPON HUMANITY?*

WOOOOOOO...

FIRST I JUDGE THAT YOU SHOULD LEAVE THE BOY **ALOOOONE!**

YOUR APPEARANCE MAKES THE NEED FOR BART SIMPSON UNNECESSARY, GREAT XT'TAPALATAKETTLE...

NOW WHAT ABOUT HUMANITY?

AND BEFORE YOU LEAVE THE SIMPSONS' HOME FOREVER, I JUDGE YOU MUST GO INSIDE THE HOUSE TO THE LAUNDRY ROOM, FIND A PAIR OF BART'S SHORTS, AND EAT THEM.

COULD WE FOCUS MORE ON THE JUDGMENT?

ALL RIGHT.

I JUDGE THAT HUMANITY *TOTALLY BLOWS.*

DUH.

WELL, THAT IS A DISAPPOINTING JUDGMENT.

OF COURSE, I WOULD BE MORE *CONCERNED* IF I SAW *THE WALL OF PURIFYING FIRE.* I DO NOT MEAN TO BE A *STICKLER,* BUT--

SNFF... SNFF...

DO YOU SMELL THAT?

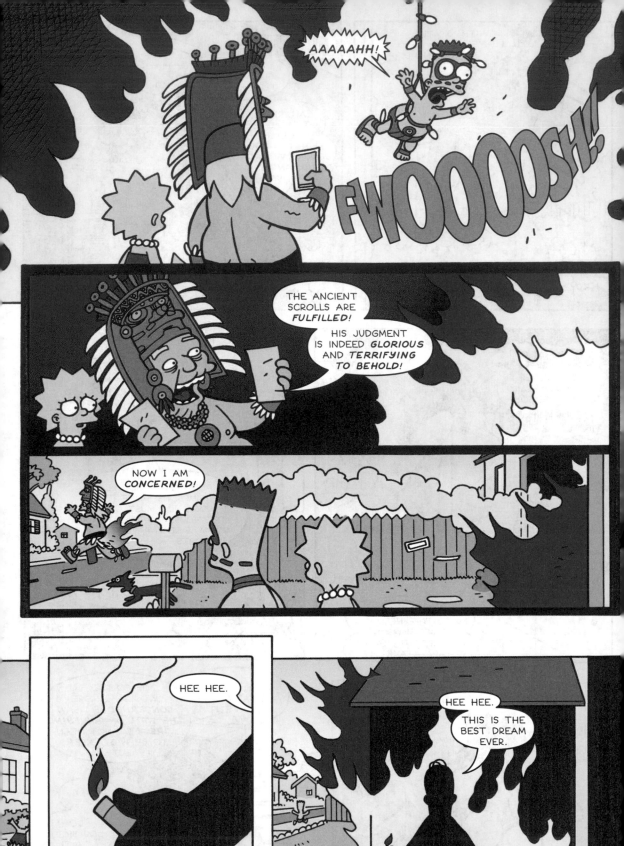

AAAAAHH!

FWOOOOSH!!

THE ANCIENT SCROLLS ARE *FULFILLED!*

HIS JUDGMENT IS INDEED *GLORIOUS* AND *TERRIFYING* TO BEHOLD!

NOW I AM *CONCERNED!*

HEE HEE.

HEE HEE.

THIS IS THE BEST DREAM EVER.

HOMER J. SIMPSON! HOW MANY TIMES ARE WE GOING TO HAVE TO GO *THROUGH* THIS?!?

I BURNED DOWN YOUR GARAGE, *FLANDERS!*

AND YOU CAN'T DO ANYTHING ABOUT IT BECAUSE I'M *DREAMING!*

IN YOUR FACE, FLANDERS!!

I CERTAINLY CAN'T STOP YOU SETTING FIRE TO MY GARAGE...

...BUT AFTER THE *THIRD* CARBONIZED CARPORT, I *DID* START BUILDING 'EM OUT OF *BALSA WOOD* AND *CARDBOARD*.

THEY PUT OUT REAL EASY, AND THEY'RE SO INEXPENSIVE TO REPLACE.

NYAAA...

IT MAKES THE WHOLE PROCESS A LOT EASIER.

...AAAAHHH!!

I QUIT!

WHAT'S THE *POINT* OF THIS DREAM IF *EVERY-THING* IS EXACTLY THE SAME AS WHEN I'M *AWAKE!!*

GGRRAAAAHHH!

DADDY, WE SAW MR. SIMPSON'S SHAME!

MR. BURNS.

THERE'S NO TIME TO BE SUBTLE. HURRY ALONG, SMITHERS.

I HAVE IN MY HANDS A CHECK FOR $750, THE COST OF A ONE-WAY TICKET TO QU'AXIALQUOTAK IN SOUTH AMERICA.

AND CAB FARE TO THE AIRPORT.

THAT'S SO GENEROUS...BUT WHY?

WE RECENTLY DISCOVERED THAT THE DODDERING ANTIQUITY STANDING BEHIND YOU IS 142-YEARS-OLD...

...MAKING HIM *THE OLDEST LIVING MAN IN SPRINGFIELD*...

...INSTEAD OF MR. BURNS.

THAT COMPLIMENTARY BIRTHDAY SWIRLEE AT PHINEAS Q. BUTTERFAT'S IS *MINE*, YOU CHURLISH PRETENDER!

6

BUT WE JUST FOUND OUT X'T'H'K'K'S AGE A FEW SECONDS AGO. HOW DID YOU--?

OH THAT. YOU WERE TALKING NEAR THE HEAD OF XT'TAPALATA-KETTLE.

I'VE PUT ELECTRONIC LISTENING DEVICES INTO *EVERY* GIFT I'VE EVER GIVEN.

IT'S *COST EFFICIENT*.

COME, SMITHERS.

TOSS ME A *COLD ONE*.

IT'S A REGULAR DUFF. I CAN'T AFFORD THE DUFF DARK.

NO, I'M GOOD. HEY, CAN I HAVE A DONUT?

KNOCK YOURSELF OUT.

MMM... ...PURPLE SPRINKLES.

I JUDGE THE WORLD TO BE *GOOD*.

YEAH. ME TOO.

THE END

I'LL JUST ꞡUNHꞡ HAMMER ꞡUHꞡ THIS **NAIL** ꞡUGHꞡ.

STUPID **MACHINE**.

I **GAVE** YOU MONEY! ALL I WANT IS MY SWEET, CHOCOLATEY **GOODNESS**!

I'VE HAD ALL OF THIS I CAN **TAKE**!

JUST ꞡUHꞡ A MOMENT WHILE I ꞡUNNHꞡ ADJUST MY ꞡNGGꞡ **GRIP**.

YOU'VE GOT IT, SIR.

ꞡUNNHꞡ ꞡNNNNGHꞡ

ꞡUHHHHꞡ

MUSN'T ꞡUNNHꞡ BLACK ꞡUHꞡ OUT--

102

FIRED? BUT *WHY?*

I HAVE A WHOLE *FILE* OF "WHYS," SIMPSON.

IT DOESN'T LOOK *THAT* THICK.

THIS IS JUST THE *INDEX!*

THE FILES ARE IN THESE *CABINETS!*

THOUSANDS OF INFRACTIONS GOING BACK *YEARS!*

I'LL JUST CLEAN OUT MY *DESK* THEN.

THAT'S *MY* DESK!

WELL, I DON'T *HAVE* ONE, OKAY?

OUT, SIMPSON!

YOU DON'T HAVE TO *YELL.* I'LL GO. ⸢SNIFF⸣

I'M LOWER THAN *LOW*. I'VE LOST MY JOB *AND* MY SELF-RESPECT.

I NEED TO TALK TO SOMEONE WHO *CARES*.

NO JOB. NO PAYCHECK. NO BEER.

BUT WE'RE *FRIENDS*, MOE!

ONLY WHEN YOUR TAB'S PAID UP, RUMMY.

COME BACK WHEN YOU'RE *EMPLOYED!*

AWWW...

IT'S *DAD*. HE'S WALKING *AWAY* FROM MOE'S AT THREE IN THE AFTERNOON...

...AND HE'S *SOBER*.

OH DEAR.

THAT CAN MEAN ONLY *ONE* THING.

YOU'VE ALREADY TRIED SNOWPLOWING, WEB HOSTING, TRUCKING, FORTUNE COOKIE WRITING, CARTOON VOICEOVERS...

...FOOD CRITIC, SCREEN-WRITER, MIXOLOGIST, BOOTLEGGER, *AND* ASTRONAUT.

MOM, WHEN'S *DINNER*?

OH *YEAH*?

AND WHO HAS TIME TO *REMEMBER* ALL OF THAT?

IT'S CALLED *CONTINUITY*.

LIVE WITH IT.

WHY DON'T *I* GET A JOB FOR A WHILE?

AND WHAT WOULD *I* DO?

YOU'D STAY *HOME* AND TAKE CARE OF THE *KIDS*.

NO WAY!

NO WIFE OF *HOMER J. SIMPSON* IS GOING TO WORK *OUTSIDE* THE HOME FOR A LIVING!

I SUPPOSE I **COULD** FIND SOME KIND OF WORK AT **HOME**.

AND CLEAN THE HOUSE AND WATCH THE KIDS.

AND..?

THEN IT'S SETTLED. **YOU'LL** WORK AT THIS OR THAT WHILE **I** EXPLORE NEW CAREER OPPORTUNITIES.

I **SUPPOSE**.

WHAT ARE YOU GONNA **DO**, MOM?

I'M NOT **SURE**, BART.

THERE ARE **PLENTY** OF HOME ENTREPRENEUR CHOICES.

CHINCHILLA RANCH. ENVELOPE STUFFING. TELEMARKETING. EXPERIMENTAL DRUG PROGRAMS.

I THINK YOU SHOULD GO WITH SOMETHING YOU **ALREADY** DO WELL, MOM.

WHAT'S **THAT**, LISA?

ISN'T IT **OBVIOUS**?

CATERING!

THE NEXT DAY...

NATIONAL CATERERS EXPO
NEXT WEEK: SMURFCON XXI

WHAT ARE THE *CHANCES* THAT THERE WOULD BE A SHOW LIKE THIS JUST AS I WAS THINKING OF BECOMING A CATERER?

I'D SAY IT'S A GOOD *SIGN*, MOM.

IT'S A WHOLE *NEW WORLD*. I'M SO *OVERWHELMED*.

WHO KNEW CATERING WAS THIS...*SHOWY*.

I'M NOT SURE IF I CAN *DO* THIS, LISA. IT'S SO MUCH *MORE* THAN FINGER FOOD AND PLASTIC CUPS.

SURE, YOU CAN, MOM. YOU JUST HAVE TO *BELIEVE*.

HRMMM...I WONDER WHERE YOUR *FATHER* IS.

BETTER *FOR* YOU THAN THE PIES THAT KRUSTY OFTEN LOBS MY WAY.

AND LESS MESSY. HEH HEH.

INANE BANTER

NOW, THE MOMENT YOU'VE ALL BEEN *HUNGERING* FOR...

...THE AWARD FOR *CATERER OF THE YEAR*. AND THE *RECIPIENT* OF THIS YEAR'S GOLDEN GANYMEADE IS...

MOVE IT ALONG...I'VE GOT A BAT MITZVAH AT THREE.

...*SPRINGFIELD'S OWN*...

...*MINDY MOREHOUSE!*

ME?

I'D LIKE TO THANK EVERYONE WHO'S EVER LIFTED A SHRIMP FORK...

YOU'VE *GOT* TO MEET HER, MOM.

I DON'T KNOW...

AFTER THE CEREMONY...

THERE SHE *IS*, MOM...*TALK* TO HER.

OH, ALL RIGHT...

...AND *THAT'S* HOW I DISCOVERED PAPRIKA.

MINDY MOREHO

MS. MOREHOUSE, I'M THINKING OF OPENING A CATERING BUSINESS *MYSELF*.

WELL, ISN'T THAT JUST *SCRUMPTIOUS!*

I WAS WONDERING...

...IF I HAD ANY *ADVICE*? *EVERYTHING* YOU NEED TO KNOW IS RIGHT IN *HERE*, MY DEAR.

MY *AUTO-BIOGRAPHY*. HOW I WENT FROM RAGS TO *RAGOUT*.

yes, I canapé

Mindy Morehouse

THANK YOU! THIS IS *VERY* GENEROUS.

OH! WELL THEN--

YES! A MERE $59.95 AND WE EXCEPT ALL MAJOR CREDIT CARDS.

AND GOOD LUCK IN YOUR NEW CONCERN. THERE'S *ALWAYS* ROOM FOR A *LITTLE COMPETITION* IN SPRINGFIELD...

...OVER MY DEAD BODY!

LADY, WHY WAS YOUR FACE ALL *SCRUNCHY*?

OH, ISN'T HE THE *CUTEST*?

JUNK. BILL. JUNK. JUNK. BILL.

WE NEVER GET ANYTHING *GOOD*.

I'M GOING TO HAVE TO GO THROUGH *FLANDERS'* MAIL AGAIN.

OH! THEY'RE *HERE*!

WHAT'S HERE?

MY BUSINESS CARDS!

HMM... SHARPER IMAGE HAS A TOOTHBRUSH THAT PLAYS CDS.

AND MY AD APPEARS TODAY IN THE NICKEL SQUEEZER.

THIS IS ONLY THE BEGINNING.

Catering by Marge
555-49...

I STILL SAY YOU SHOULD HAVE BOUGHT A SUPER BOWL SPOT.

SURE. GREAT IDEA, HOMER.

THAT WAS SARCASM, RIGHT?

THAT WAS SARCASM, RIGHT?

OH NO, HONEY. I MEANT THAT.

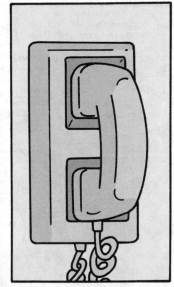

MOM, YOU'VE BEEN STARING AT THE PHONE FOR HOURS.

I GOT TIRED OF WATCHING THE POTS NOT BOILING.

WHO AM I KIDDING? NO ONE IS EVER GOING TO CALL.

CHEER UP, MOM. I'LL BET THERE'S SOMEONE THINKING OF HIRING YOU RIGHT THIS MINUTE.

MEANWHILE...

I WON'T **DO** IT!

BUT, *RAINIER!*

CASA D
WOLFCAS

YOU HAVE A "*COMMITMENT* TO DO *MCBAIN XIII: RETURN TO MCBAIN III.*"

YOU'RE *GREENLIT* TO DIRECT THE NON-MUSICAL RE-MAKE OF "*THE SOUND OF MUSIC.*"

AND WE *SOLD* THE PILOT FOR "*POLICE MONKEY*"!

I AM *THROUGH* WITH ALL THAT!

I AM A *SERIOUS ACTOR!* I WANT TO *STRETCH* MY MUSCLES!

MY *ACTING* MUSCLES!

BUT THE PUBLIC ONLY *LIKES* YOU WHEN YOU'RE A *ROBOT!*

OR *SHOOTING* PEOPLE!

OR SHOOTING *ROBOTS!*

THIS IS THE MOVIE I WISH TO MAKE NEXT!

IT IS A *SENSITIVE PORTRAIT* OF A MAN DEALING WITH THE *FAILED RELATIONSHIPS* OF HIS LIFE.

I PET *BUNNIES* AND SIP *LATTES* IN THE PARISIAN RAIN.

Tender Kisses in the SHADOWS

I *WILL* MAKE THIS MOVIE OR SOMEONE WILL *PAY!*

POUND!

115

"THIS IS A *NIGHTMARE!*"

Mindy Morehouse

OOOO!

--A BIG PAHTY WITH *MANY CELEBRITIES* AND CATERING BY MAHGE SIMPSON.

WHAT'S *WRONG,* MINDY?

WHAT'S *NOT* WRONG?

THE *BIGGEST EVENT* OF THE *SPRING-FIELD SOCIAL CALENDAR,* AND THAT *UPSTART* IS DOING THE FOOD PREP!

I'M SO *ANGRY* YOU COULD SAUTÉE A BRIE-FILLED CREPE LIGHTLY SPICED WITH SAGE AND SERVED WITH A PLUM SAUCE ON MY FOREHEAD!

BUT YOUR REPUTATION IS SECURE.

THIS SIMPSON CHICK *COULD* SCREW UP.

WHY LEAVE IT TO *CHANCE?*

I THINK IT'S TIME TO *SEASON* THIS *RECIPE FOR DISASTER.*

KIDS! YOU'RE JUST IN TIME TO HELP!

MOM'S FREAKING OUT!

WHAT IS IT, MOM?

RAINIERWOLFCASTLECALLED ANDWEHAVETOMAKEENOUGH FOODFORSIXHUNDREDPEOPLE IN48HOURS!

A CATERING JOB AT LAST!

RAINIER WOLFCASTLE IS ON "48 HOURS"?

BART CAN OPEN THE CANS OF PATÉ AND WHIP THE EGGS FOR QUICHE HORS' D'OEUVRES.

LISA CAN ROLL THE CREPES AND ZEST THE LEMONS.

HOMER CAN RUN DOWN TO BUYMORE AND PICK UP THE REST OF THE STUFF I NEED.

AND I CAN...

...MAKE ANOTHER FOUR GALLONS OF POTATO SALAD.

HRMMM...

WHAT?

FORTY HOURS LATER...

I CAN'T BELIEVE IT, BUT WE'RE FINALLY DONE.

AND THINK OF THE LEFTOVERS.

MMM...LEFT-OVERS.

GAAAAH...

WHO... WHO *REVIVED* ME?

ME ₅PTUH₅ MR. BURNS ₅PUH!₅

YES! *YES!*

HOW MIGHT I *REPAY* YOU FOR STAVING OFF MY ETERNAL REST YET AGAIN?

DONE.

UM...HOW ABOUT A *JOB* AT THE NUCLEAR PLANT?

NO! *NO!*

YOU'RE THE *CATERER?* YOU CAN USE YOUR TUPPERWARE TO HOLD ALL THE *LAWSUITS* COMING YOUR WAY!

BUT...I DON'T *UNDERSTAND.*

YOU *POISONED* YOUR CLIENT'S GUESTS, MARGE.

MINDY MOREHOUSE, WHY ARE *YOU* HERE?

TO *GLOAT,* OF COURSE.

WHAT KIND OF PERSON *DOES* THAT?

HAW HAW!

YOU'RE *ARRESTING* ME?

WE *FROWN* ON FOLKS SPIKING THE H'ORS D'OEUVRES AROUND HERE, LADY.

BUT MOM IS *INNOCENT!*

SIMPSON! ≥SOB!≥ SIMPSON!

WHO IS THIS *SIMPSON* YOU'RE ON ABOUT?

SIX MONTHS LATER...

WORLD PREMIERE: McBAIN XIV: THE BIG HURL

SORRY WE KILLED YOUR *FAMILY*, MCBAIN!

"SORRY" DOESN'T CURE THE *TROTS*, BABY.

NOT *THAT!*

OH *NO!* THE *BIG* HURL!

HROOOP!

GREAT PERFORMANCE, RAINIER! *LINDA BLAIR* GREAT!

AREN'T YOU *GLAD* YOU PASSED ON THAT CHICK FLICK?

YOU'RE *BACK*, BABY!

"YOU'RE BACK, BABY." I *LIKE* IT!

THE END!